MACBOOK PRO WITH M4 CHIPS USER GUIDE

macOS Sequoia Features, Setup Instructions, Troubleshooting, Apple M4 Chip Benefits, and Battery Management Tips' Manual for Beginners and Seniors

By

Tatiana Dash

CONTENTS

INTRODUCTION

Overview of the New MacBook Pro M4 series

Apple's latest MacBook Pro, featuring the M4 family of chips (M4, M4 Pro, M4 Max), is built for high performance with powerful new capabilities. It includes Apple Intelligence, a new personal intelligence system designed to enhance productivity and protect privacy.

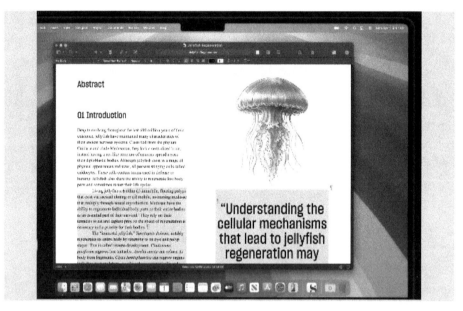

The new models are available in 14- and 16-inch sizes with a Liquid Retina XDR display, an advanced 12MP Center Stage camera, up to 24-hour battery life, and Thunderbolt 5 on M4 Pro and M4 Max models for fast connectivity.

The M4 family offers impressive advancements, such as superior single- and multi-threaded performance, enhanced machine learning, and up to 128GB unified memory on M4 Max. These chips allow for seamless handling of large projects and demanding tasks. macOS Sequoia further boosts user experience with features like iPhone Mirroring, Safari Highlights, and a Passwords app, making it ideal for upgraders, with eco-friendly construction and up to 10x faster performance over Intel-based models.

The excitement surrounding the MacBook Pro M4 series is palpable—and it's entirely justified! Apple's new M4 Pro and M4 Max processors set a stunning benchmark for speed, efficiency, and intelligence. In this era of Apple's relentless innovation, the MacBook Pro with M4 isn't just a laptop; it's an advanced powerhouse designed for creators, developers, and professionals who crave seamless performance without limits.

First, imagine the sheer power packed into the new M4 chips. With their sophisticated neural engines and enhanced cores, they redefine multitasking and graphics performance, making demanding software—from video editing in Final Cut Pro to 3D rendering in Blender—feel effortless. The M4 Max, especially, pushes boundaries with extra GPU cores and memory bandwidth, ideal for those working with large files, intense visuals, and heavy-duty simulations. Whether you're editing 8K video or running complex code, the M4 Max is crafted to handle it all with blazing speed.

The new MacBook Pro's design also complements this performance. Sporting an elegant, slim profile with enhanced cooling systems, it's built to sustain high speeds without overheating. The gorgeous Liquid Retina XDR display offers stunning colour accuracy, peak brightness, and dynamic range, ideal for photographers, designers, and creatives seeking an immersive experience. With ProMotion's adaptive refresh rate, every animation and scroll feels smooth and responsive.

And let's talk about battery life: Apple's move to M4 means even more energy efficiency, so you can push through longer work sessions without constantly reaching for the charger. Plus, with new macOS Sequoia, the system leverages the M4's intelligence with advanced AI-driven features that adapt to your workflow, manage resources smartly, and enhance security.

In short, the Apple MacBook Pro with M4 is a glimpse into the future of personal computing, where performance meets intelligence seamlessly. You're right to be eagerly waiting; this release is bound to raise the bar for what a professional laptop can achieve.

While the Macbook Pro **M4** comes with an entry-level chip with 10 core CPU and 10-core GPU, the **M4 Pro** and **M4 Max** models are both part of Apple's advanced M4 series that offer exceptional powerful performance upgrades with significant differences tailored for various user needs,

Differences between M4 Pro and M4 Max Models

1. Performance and Core Configuration:

M4 Pro: Comes with a 14-core CPU (10 performance cores, 4 efficiency cores) and up to a 20-core GPU. This model supports up to 64GB of unified memory, with a memory bandwidth of 273GB/s, which is ideal for multitasking and productivity tasks.

M4 Max: Takes performance further with a 16-core CPU (12 performance cores, 4 efficiency cores) and a 40-core GPU, allowing it to handle the most demanding graphical tasks. It supports up to 128GB of unified memory with a bandwidth of 546GB/s, which is excellent for heavy computational work and professional-grade video editing.

2. Graphics and Video Capabilities:

The **M4 Max** shines in video and graphics processing, with dual video encode engines and ProRes accelerators, providing real-time performance for tasks like RAW footage de-noising in software like DaVinci Resolve Studio. This makes it the go-to choice for video professionals needing high GPU power.

3. Battery Life:

Due to its efficiency cores and optimized design, the **M4 Pro** model generally offers longer battery life than the M4 Max. For instance, the 16-inch M4 Pro model can last up to 24 hours for video streaming, compared to 21 hours for the M4 Max.

4. Pricing and Target Audience:

M4 Pro models are priced starting from $1,999 and cater to users looking for high performance with extended battery life and excellent multitasking capabilities. The **M4 Max**, at a premium, is tailored for professionals who require extreme performance, especially in graphics-intensive fields like video editing, 3D rendering, and machine learning.

These distinctions make the M4 Pro ideal for power users seeking a balance of performance and efficiency, while the M4 Max is suited for intensive workloads that demand the highest level of computational power and graphics. Both models feature the new Thunderbolt 5 connectivity, 12MP Center Stage camera, and Liquid Retina XDR display, underscoring Apple's commitment to top-notch technology across the board.

Benefits of Owning MacBook Pro (M4 Pro) or (M4 Max)

The MacBook Pro **M4 Pro** and **M4 Max** models offer top-tier performance improvements and cutting-edge features that will excite anyone that it is doing to me, here's a rundown of what I think makes them awesome devices to buy:

1. Next-Gen Processing Power

Both the **M4 Pro** and **M4 Max** chips showcase Apple's most advanced silicon, designed for peak performance in both CPU and GPU tasks. They parade what has been described as a powerful mix of performance and efficiency cores, with the M4 Max reaching up to **16 CPU cores** (12 performance and 4 efficiency cores) and **40 GPU cores**, making it ideal for high-end applications like video editing and machine learning.

Compared to previous models, both chips offer increased processing efficiency and speed, which results in better power usage and less heat generation, keeping the MacBook **cooler** during intensive tasks.

2. Enhanced Graphics and Ray Tracing

The GPUs in the M4 series got significantly upgraded ray-tracing capabilities, that has been ascertained would offer up to **2x faster ray tracing** over prior models. This is particularly beneficial for professionals working in graphic design, gaming, or any graphics-intensive applications.

The M4 Max takes this a step further with additional cores and memory bandwidth that will provide a rich experience for creators handling heavy 3D modelling or rendering workloads.

3. Advanced Memory and Storage Options

We have also been told that the **M4 Pro** supports up to **64GB of unified memory** with a bandwidth of 273GB/s, whereas the **M4 Max** goes further with **128GB of unified memory** and a staggering 546GB/s bandwidth. This expansive memory allows both models to handle data-heavy applications effortlessly, giving users an edge in multitasking and running AI and large language models without latency.

These amazing memory configurations make the M4 Max especially suitable for developers and data scientists who need high-bandwidth data transfer for demanding workloads.

4. Thunderbolt 5 and Connectivity

For the first time, Apple's MacBook Pro models now support **Thunderbolt 5**, which will allow up to **120Gb/s data transfer speeds**. This, of course, opens up possibilities for faster connections to external drives, multiple displays, and other peripherals that will surely enhance productivity.

5. AI and Machine Learning Performance

The M4 chips have advanced machine-learning accelerators, making them highly efficient in handling AI tasks. For example, the **M4 Max** is capable of processing massive AI models with up to 200 billion parameters, benefiting developers and researchers working on deep learning and neural networks.

6. Professional Video Processing

With **dual video encode engines** and dedicated ProRes accelerators, the M4 Max is tailored for video professionals. It efficiently handles RAW footage, allowing real-time processing in demanding video editing software, making it a powerhouse for filmmakers and content creators.

Overall, the M4 Pro and M4 Max MacBook Pros deliver groundbreaking performance that would excite anyone interested in Apple technology.

System requirements and compatibility

The MacBook Pro M4 series centres on Apple's latest hardware and macOS features, specifically designed to support intensive tasks and seamless integration across Apple devices. Here are the key elements:

macOS Compatibility: Both the M4 Pro and M4 Max models require the latest macOS version, which is macOS Sequoia which is optimized to leverage the new M4 chip architecture. This setup ensures that users benefit from improved AI-driven performance, enhanced power efficiency, and Apple's high-level security protocols.

1. **External Display and Peripheral Support**:

The **M4 Pro** can handle up to two external displays with Thunderbolt 5 connectivity, a significant upgrade for professional users needing high-speed data transfer (up to 120 Gbps).

The **M4 Max** supports up to four external displays, ideal for those requiring multi-screen setups for design, video editing, or large-scale presentations.

2. **Memory and Storage Options**:

The M4 Pro starts with a minimum of 24GB unified memory, configurable up to 48GB, while the M4 Max offers a more robust option of up to 128GB, accommodating tasks such as 3D rendering and heavy data analysis.

Both models feature storage options that begin at 512GB SSD, expandable up to 8TB on the M4 Max, which benefits users working with large files or media libraries.

Software and Application Compatibility: The M4 series is built to support professional-grade software like Final Cut Pro, Adobe Creative Cloud, Xcode, and other performance-intensive applications. This compatibility, combined with macOS optimizations, enables faster processing times and a smoother workflow.

Ecosystem Integration: These models are highly compatible with Apple's ecosystem, supporting AirDrop, Handoff, and Sidecar, allowing users to use devices like iPads as secondary displays or integrate seamlessly with other Apple hardware.

Battery and Performance Requirements: These MacBook Pros are designed with battery efficiency in mind, allowing for longer work periods on a single charge without compromising performance.

INITIAL SETUP

Here's a guide for setting up your new MacBook Pro M4 series:

1. Unboxing Your MacBook Pro Safely

- **Open the Box Carefully**: Place the box on a stable, flat surface. Use a small knife or scissors to cut any seals gently. Avoid excessive force to prevent damaging any items inside.

- **Remove Components One at a Time**: As you open, take out each item carefully, including your MacBook Pro, power adapter, and USB-C cable. Keep the packaging for any potential returns or repairs.

2. Accessories Included

- **MacBook Pro Device**: The main device, wrapped securely for protection.

- **USB-C Power Adapter and Charging Cable**: Typically included is a 96W or 140W USB-C adapter depending on the model.

- **Documentation**: A quick start guide, regulatory information, and Apple stickers may also be in the box.

3. Setting Up for the First Time

- **Powering On the Device**: Open the MacBook lid, which may power it on automatically. If not, press the power button in the top-right corner of the keyboard.

Initial Configurations:

Language, Region, and Time Zone: When the setup assistant appears, choose your language, region, and time zone. This will help optimize settings based on your location.

Connecting to Wi-Fi: Select your Wi-Fi network and enter the password to connect. An internet connection is essential for account setup and software updates.

click the Wi-Fi button 🛜
to see your preferred networks

Sign In with Apple ID: To sync your apps, settings, and data, sign in with your Apple ID. If you don't have one, you can create it during setup.

Follow the Setup Steps to Create a New Apple ID: You'll be prompted to enter your name, birthday, and email address (or create a new iCloud email) and set a password. Then, follow the steps for setting up security questions or verifying a phone number.

Verify Your Email: If you're using an existing email, Apple will send a verification code to confirm it's yours.

Set Up iCloud

- Once you're signed in, you'll see a prompt asking if you'd like to use **iCloud**.

- Enable iCloud to sync and back up essential data (contacts, photos, app data, and more) across your Apple devices.

- You'll have the option to toggle specific iCloud features, like **Photos, iCloud Drive**, **Notes**, and **Messages**.

Enable "Find My Macbook" Enabling **Find My** device helps you locate your Macbook Pro if it's ever lost or stolen. Simply tap **Find My Macbook** under the iCloud settings and toggle it to on.

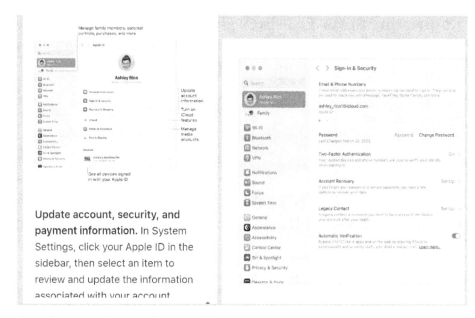

Update account, security, and payment information. In System Settings, click your Apple ID in the sidebar, then select an item to review and update the information associated with your account

Setting Up Security Options:

Password: Set a secure password for logging into your MacBook.

Note: Your computer account is not the same as your Apple ID, though if you ever forget the password to unlock your Mac, you can use your Apple ID to reset the password if you check this option during setup.

Touch ID: For models with Touch ID, you can set it up by following on-screen prompts. Place your finger on the Touch ID sensor repeatedly until the scan completes.

Touch ID (power button)

Function (Fn)/Globe key

Touch ID

Set up Touch ID. You can set up Touch ID during setup, or at a later

Face ID: Although Face ID isn't currently available on MacBook Pro models, ensure your MacBook has up-to-date security by enabling features like FileVault for data encryption and iCloud Keychain for password management.

4. Additional Initial Configurations

System Preferences and Updates: After the initial setup, go to System Preferences to adjust the display, trackpad, and keyboard settings to your liking.

Software Update: Ensure you're on the latest macOS version by navigating to **System Preferences > Software Update** and installing any available updates for optimal performance and security.

Once these steps are complete, your MacBook Pro will be ready to use! Setting up these configurations initially will ensure smooth functionality and a more personalized experience.

MacBook Pro Hardware Overview

The MacBook Pro M4 models have been designed with both functionality and a sleek, minimalist style, equipped with a variety of ports for connectivity and ease of use. Here's a quick look at the main physical features and ports:

Physical Features and Ports

Display and Bezels: The MacBook Pro models feature edge-to-edge Liquid Retina XDR displays, known for high brightness levels, rich colours, and contrast. The bezel is ultra-thin, allowing for an immersive visual experience.

Keyboard and Trackpad: Apple's Magic Keyboard comes with a redesigned scissor mechanism that provides a quiet yet responsive typing experience. Below the keyboard, the spacious Force Touch trackpad supports pressure-sensitive tasks, multitouch gestures, and haptic feedback.

Power Button

Location and Functionality: The power button is located at the top-right corner of the keyboard, doubling as a **Touch ID sensor**.

Touch ID Integration: This fingerprint sensor can be used for unlocking the laptop, authorizing payments, and authenticating passwords securely, making access both quick and secure.

Thunderbolt / USB-C Ports

Thunderbolt 5 (on M4 Pro and M4 Max): Both M4 Pro and M4 Max models are equipped with multiple Thunderbolt 5 ports, supporting high-speed data transfers up to 120 Gbps. This is useful for users needing fast connections to external devices like hard drives, monitors, and eGPUs.

USB-C Compatibility: These ports are compatible with USB-C, allowing connections to a wide range of USB-C devices and accessories for added versatility.

HDMI Port

4K and 8K Support: The HDMI 2.1 port supports external displays up to 4K at 240Hz and 8K at 60Hz on the M4 Max models, which makes it ideal for video editing, streaming, or extended displays in professional setups.

SD Card Slot

UHS-II SD Card Support: Ideal for photographers and videographers, the SD card slot on the M4 Pro and M4 Max supports UHS-II, allowing for fast data transfers directly from SD cards, which is convenient for handling large media files.

Audio Jack and Other Ports

3.5mm Headphone Jack: The MacBook Pro includes a 3.5mm audio jack, now enhanced to support high-impedance headphones. This is valuable for audiophiles and professionals who rely on high-quality audio monitoring.

MagSafe 4: Apple has reintroduced MagSafe for the M4 models, with faster charging capabilities and a magnetic connection that safely detaches if pulled.

These hardware features give users a balanced experience of power, speed, and connectivity.

Keyboard and Trackpad

The MacBook Pro M4 keyboard and trackpad are designed to support an efficient and fluid workflow, especially for creative and professional users. Below is a breakdown of their main features, functionality, and customization options.

MacBook Pro Keyboard

The keyboard in the M4 series retains Apple's **Magic Keyboard** design, which features a refined scissor mechanism to ensure stability, quiet typing, and a responsive feel.

- **Shortcut Keys and Function Keys**:

Function Keys: Depending on your MacBook Pro model, the function keys along the top row (F1 to F12) allow you to control essential functions like volume, brightness, playback, and more. These keys also support shortcuts for tasks like opening Mission Control (F3), adjusting keyboard brightness (F5, F6), and launching Siri (F10).

Shortcut Keys: macOS offers a range of keyboard shortcuts to streamline your workflow. For example, **Command + C** for copy, **Command + V** for paste, and **Command + Tab** to switch between open applications. You can view or customize these shortcuts in **System Settings > Keyboard**.

- **Touch Bar (if applicable)**:

The **Touch Bar** (available on some previous models, but phased out in recent releases) provides dynamic controls that adapt based on the app you're using. For example, when using Safari, you can use the Touch Bar for functions like adding bookmarks or switching tabs.

Touch ID: The **Touch ID** sensor, located at the top-right corner, allows for quick unlocking, secure app access, and fast Apple Pay authentication.

MacBook Pro Trackpad

The MacBook Pro's **Force Touch Trackpad** supports pressure-sensitive feedback and multi-touch gestures that make navigating and interacting with macOS intuitive and efficient.

Using Gestures:

- **Click**: A single press to select or open an item.

- **Force Click**: A deeper press provides additional functionality, like previewing a file in Finder or opening a dictionary definition for selected text.

- **Two-Finger Swipe**: Move two fingers up or down to scroll, or left/right to navigate back and forward in browsers.

- **Pinch and Zoom**: Pinch with two fingers to zoom in or out of documents, photos, or websites.

- **Three-Finger Swipe**: Swipe up with three fingers to open Mission Control, or swipe down for App Exposé.

- **Four-Finger Swipe Left/Right**: Swipe between full-screen apps or desktop spaces.

Gesture	Action		
	Click: Press anywhere on the trackpad. Or enable "Tap to click" in Trackpad Settings, and simply tap.	↑↑ ⇓⇓	Two-finger scroll: Slide two fingers up or down to scroll.
	Force click: Click and then press deeper. You can use force click to look up more information—click a word to see its definition, or an address to see a preview that you can open in Maps.		Pinch to zoom: Pinch your thumb and finger open or closed to zoom in or out of photos and webpages.
	Secondary click (that is, right-click): Click with two fingers to open shortcut menus. If "Tap to click" is enabled, tap with two fingers. On the keyboard, press the Control key and click the trackpad.	⟵⟶ ⟵⟶	Swipe to navigate: Swipe left or right with two fingers to flip through webpages, documents, and more—like turning a page in a book.
			Open Launchpad: Quickly open apps in Launchpad. Pinch closed with four or five fingers, then click an app to open it.

Swipe between apps: To switch from one full-screen app to another, swipe left or right with three or four fingers.

Customizing Trackpad Settings:

Access **System Settings > Trackpad** to adjust tracking speed, enable secondary click (right-click), and turn on/off gestures. You can enable or disable features like "Tap to click" or adjust tracking speed for smoother cursor movement.

MACOS SEQUOIA

macOS Sequoia, the latest macOS version, builds on Apple's tradition of integrating powerful performance with user-friendly design and advanced AI features. This version is designed to harness the full capabilities of Apple Silicon, specifically optimized for the M4 Pro and M4 Max chips. Here's a few things you need to know about what makes macOS Sequoia distinct:

1. Enhanced Performance and Power Management

- **Apple Silicon Optimization**: Sequoia is tailored for M4 chips, maximizing speed and efficiency, especially when handling intensive tasks like rendering, video editing, and multitasking.

- **Intelligent Power Management**: Thanks to optimized chip and OS integration, Sequoia provides longer battery life, dynamically adjusting power consumption based on task requirements.

2. Advanced AI and Machine Learning

- **Smart Automation**: New AI-driven features like Smart Automation help users streamline daily workflows. For example, AI in Sequoia can suggest actions based on previous tasks, such as organizing files or launching specific applications.

- **On-device Machine Learning**: Enhanced machine learning algorithms now run directly on the device, enabling faster, more private data processing and support for advanced apps in areas like photography, productivity and creative work.

3. Redesigned User Interface

- **Refined Aesthetics**: The interface in Sequoia has a modern, minimalist look with improved transparency effects and streamlined menu designs.

- **Dynamic Widgets and Interactive Control Center**: Widgets are now more customizable and interactive, providing live information and allowing quick actions directly from the desktop or control centre.

4. Seamless Ecosystem Integration

- **Universal Control Enhancements**: Improvements to Universal Control make it easier to work across multiple Apple devices, allowing users to drag and drop files, type, and navigate seamlessly between MacBook, iPad, and even iPhone screens.

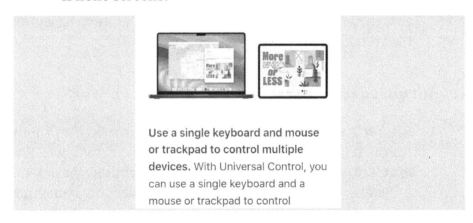

Use a single keyboard and mouse or trackpad to control multiple devices. With Universal Control, you can use a single keyboard and a mouse or trackpad to control

- **Sidecar Updates**: Sidecar lets iPads act as secondary displays, with faster response times and enhanced touch support for graphic design, presentations, and multitasking.

5. Security and Privacy

- **Enhanced Security Features**: Sequoia includes upgraded encryption, improved firewall protections, and enhanced features for Safari's Private Browsing to ensure a secure internet experience.

- **Data Privacy Controls**: The OS provides greater transparency around data use by applications, and users have more granular control over what data apps can access.

6. Customization Options

- **Control Center Customization**: Users can now personalize the Control Center with quick-access toggles for the features they use most.

- **Focus Modes and Widgets**: Enhanced Focus Modes allow users to create customized work, personal, and relaxation modes, with widgets adjusting automatically based on the mode selected.

In short, macOS Sequoia is designed to support productivity, creativity, and security in a streamlined, powerful, and highly personalizable OS, which now appears to be a new standard for Mac users.

System Preferences and customization

Here's how to navigate **System Preferences** (now called **System Settings** in the latest version of macOS) to customize key settings on your MacBook Pro M4 series:

1. Changing Wallpaper and Adjusting Display Settings

- **Wallpaper**:

Go to **System Settings > Wallpaper**. Here, you can choose from a variety of dynamic wallpapers, Apple's default images, or even add your own custom images.

Dynamic wallpapers adjust based on the time of day, creating a visually engaging experience that changes from morning to evening.

- **Display Settings**:

System Settings > Displays allows you to adjust **brightness**, enable **True Tone** to adapt colours based on ambient light and turn on **Night Shift** to reduce blue light exposure in the evening.

For external monitors, use the same section to manage **resolution** and **refresh rates**, particularly helpful if you're connecting to a 4K or higher display.

2. Configuring Battery and Power Settings

- Go to **System Settings** > **Battery** to customize how your MacBook uses power and prolong battery life.

- **Optimized Battery Charging**: This feature learns your charging habits and adapts to help reduce wear on the battery by pausing charging at 80% until you need a full charge.

- **Low Power Mode**: Enabling Low Power Mode can help extend battery life by lowering screen brightness and limiting background activities.

- **Power Adapter Settings**: If you often use your MacBook plugged in, select "Battery Health" under the battery settings to optimize the charging cycles, keeping your battery healthy over time.

3. Customizing the Dock and Menu Bar

- **Dock Customization**:

Go to **System Settings** > **Dock & Menu Bar** to adjust the Dock size, magnification, and positioning on the screen. You can also choose to auto-hide the Dock when not in use.

The Dock, at the bottom of the screen, is a convenient place to keep the apps and documents you use frequently.

Recently opened apps appear in the center section of the Dock.

Enable the "Minimize windows into application icon" option to reduce Dock clutter by keeping minimized windows grouped.

- **Menu Bar Customization**:

The **Dock & Menu Bar** section also lets you adjust menu bar items, deciding which icons appear in the top-right corner.

For quick access to frequently used items, enable icons for **Battery**, **Wi-Fi**, **Bluetooth**, and **Do Not Disturb**.

Widgets and controls like sound and brightness can be dragged into or out of the menu bar, tailoring the experience to your needs.

Customizing these settings can make your MacBook Pro M4 not only visually pleasing but also optimized for your specific usage needs, extending battery life and improving functionality.

How to Set Up Multiple Users and User Accounts

Creating separate user accounts on your MacBook Pro is useful if the device is shared among multiple people. Here's a guide on how to set it up and manage your accounts:

1. **Go to System Settings**:
   - Open **System Settings** and select **Users & Groups**.
2. **Add a New User**:
   - Click the **Add Account** button (usually a "+" icon) to create a new account.
   - You'll need to enter an **Admin password** to authorize this action if you're not already logged in as an admin.
3. **Choose Account Type**:

      ○   Select the account type you want to create:

Admin: Has full access to the system and can add or remove other users.

Standard: Can use the Mac but cannot make changes that affect other users.

Managed with Parental Controls: Useful for children, where parents can limit access to certain apps or set time restrictions.

Sharing Only: For users who only need access to shared files remotely without full access to the Mac.

4. **Set Up Login Details**:

Enter a **name, account name, and password** for the new user. You can also add a **password hint** if needed.

5. **Customizing User Settings**:

Once the account is set up, you can set profile images and manage permissions in **Users & Groups** for each user.

To switch between accounts, go to the **Apple menu > Log Out** or use **Fast User Switching** from the menu bar, if enabled.

Using Accessibility Settings and Options

macOS offers extensive accessibility options to accommodate users with various needs. Here's an overview of how to enable and adjust these features:

1. **Accessing Accessibility Settings**:

Open **System Settings** and select **Accessibility** to see a range of options organized into categories like Vision, Hearing, Physical and Motor, and General.

2. **Vision Accessibility Options**:

VoiceOver: A screen reader that provides spoken descriptions of what's on your screen, including text and controls. Enable it in **Accessibility > VoiceOver**.

Zoom: Magnifies portions of the screen for better visibility. Go to **Accessibility > Zoom** to activate it and customize magnification levels.

Display: Adjust settings for **contrast, cursor size, and colour filters**. You can reduce transparency or invert colours to make the display easier to view.

3. **Hearing Accessibility Options**:

Audio: Turn on Mono Audio to play both channels of stereo audio through one speaker, helpful for users with hearing loss in one ear.

Subtitles & Closed Captions: macOS supports captions for media content. Customize text size, font, and background color under **Accessibility > Captions**.

4. **Physical and Motor Accessibility Options**:

AssistiveTouch: If using a mouse or trackpad is challenging, enable AssistiveTouch to create shortcuts for gestures and actions.

Voice Control: Allows users to navigate and control the Mac with voice commands, set up under **Accessibility > Voice Control**.

Keyboard Accessibility: Customize features like Slow Keys and Sticky Keys under **Keyboard**, which adjust how key presses are interpreted, useful for users with motor difficulties.

5. General Accessibility Options:

Siri and Dictation: Voice control through **Siri** and dictation enables hands-free operation, helpful for quick tasks and searches.

Pointer Control: Under **Accessibility > Pointer Control**, you can adjust the size and colour of the mouse pointer and enable settings like Shake to Locate, which enlarges the pointer when you shake the mouse.

These accessibility settings allow you to tailor the Mac experience to meet diverse needs.

USING MACOS SEQUOIA CORE FUNCTIONALITIES

Here's a guide to help you get the most out of macOS Sequoia's core functions, including desktop navigation, file organization, and iCloud integration.

1. Navigating the Desktop and Finder

- **Desktop**:

The desktop in macOS is where you can store files, folders, and shortcuts for easy access. It provides quick access to frequently used items and has a flexible layout that you can organize according to your needs.

Use **Stacks** to keep your desktop tidy. This feature automatically groups similar file types, such as documents or images, into stacks, reducing desktop clutter.

- **Finder**:
    - Finder is macOS's file management interface, where you can browse and organize files. Open Finder from the **Dock** (the icon with a blue face).
    - Use the **Sidebar** for quick access to folders, including **Applications**, **Documents**, **Downloads**, and external drives.
    - **Toolbar** options like viewing files as icons, lists, or columns make navigating through folders easier. You can also customize the toolbar by right-clicking on it and adding frequently used tools.

2. *File Organization and Management*

- **Creating Folders**:
    - To create a folder, right-click (or Control-click) on the desktop or in a Finder window and select **New Folder**. You can also use the shortcut **Command + Shift + N**.
    - Rename a folder by clicking its name, and then typing a new name.

- **Organizing Files**:
    - **Tagging Files**: Right-click on a file and choose a colour tag to categorize files, making them easy to locate via **Finder's Sidebar** or **Spotlight Search**.
    - **Grouping and Sorting**: Finder allows you to sort files by name, date, size, and kind. You can adjust this by selecting **View > Sort By** or by clicking the column headers in the list view.

- **Deleting Files**:

  - Drag files to the **Trash** or right-click and select **Move to Trash**. To permanently delete, go to **Finder > Empty Trash**.

  - For recently deleted files, the **Trash** folder allows you to recover items if needed before they're permanently removed.

3. Using iCloud Drive for Storage and Backup

- **Setting Up iCloud Drive**:

  - Go to **System Settings > Apple ID > iCloud Drive**. From here, toggle **iCloud Drive** on and select which folders you want to sync.

  - iCloud automatically backs up your Desktop and Documents folders if you enable them. This ensures that files stored in these folders are accessible on all Apple devices linked to the same Apple ID.

- **File Management with iCloud**:

  - Files stored in iCloud can be accessed from Finder under the **iCloud Drive** section. You can create new folders, organize files, and even collaborate on documents with other Apple users through **iCloud Drive sharing**.

  - **Optimized Storage**: If you're low on storage space, **Optimized Storage** moves older files to iCloud, keeping them accessible without using up local storage. Enable it by going to **System Settings > Apple ID > iCloud > Optimize Mac Storage**.

Understanding and Using macOS Features

These arguably are some of the most useful features in macOS-features like Spotlight **Search**, **Quick Look**, **Mission Control and Spaces**, and **Widgets and Notification Center**.

1. Spotlight Search

Spotlight is the powerful, built-in search tool in macOS that allows you to quickly find files, apps, emails, web results, and more directly from your desktop.

How to Use:

- Press Command + Space or click the magnifying glass icon in the top-right corner to open Spotlight.

- Type your query, and Spotlight will provide relevant results, such as documents, images, settings, and even definitions or calculations.

Spotlight is not just a file search; it integrates with online search and Siri Suggestions, allowing you to search the web, get weather updates, or do quick conversions, all without opening a browser.

2. *Quick Look*

Quick Look allows you to preview files without opening them fully, saving time when browsing files.

To Use this:

- Select a file in Finder and press the Spacebar to open a Quick Look preview. You can view images, documents, PDFs, and even video files this way.
- To expand the preview to full screen, click the expand **button** in the Quick Look window.

Quick Look supports a wide range of file types and even allows some basic edits, like trimming videos or rotating images, making it highly efficient for quick file inspection and organization.

3. Mission Control and Spaces

Mission Control helps manage open windows and desktops (Spaces), making multitasking and navigation across multiple tasks more organized.

How to Use:

- Access Mission Control by swiping up with three fingers on the trackpad or pressing the **F3 key** (or a custom shortcut).
- You'll see an overview of all open windows, allowing you to switch between them easily.
- At the top of the screen, you can create additional desktops (Spaces) for different workflows. Drag an app to a specific Space to organize tasks across virtual desktops.

Mission Control and Spaces keep your workspace uncluttered, letting you organize apps and documents by project or task type, which can boost productivity.

4. Widgets and Notification Center

Widgets and Notification Center provide quick access to updates and information without disrupting your main workspace.

Notification Center: Click the **date and time** in the top-right corner to open the Notification Center, which shows recent notifications and calendar events.

Click to open Notification Center.

Widgets: In the Notification Center, scroll to the bottom and click **Edit Widgets** to customize what's displayed. Available widgets include weather, reminders, stocks, calendar events, and more.

You can interact with widgets (e.g., mark reminders as complete) directly from the Notification Center.

Widgets provide useful at-a-glance information, while the Notification Center helps you keep track of notifications in an organized panel, making it easy to stay updated without interrupting your workflow.

APPLICATIONS AND SOFTWARE ESSENTIALS ON MACOS

macOS comes with a suite of pre-installed apps for essential functions, access to additional software via the App Store, and support for third-party applications. Here's a comprehensive look at these elements:

1. Pre-installed macOS Apps

These are a range of built-in apps designed to support everyday tasks and enhance productivity:

- **Safari**: Safari is Apple's fast and efficient web browser, with features like Reading List, iCloud integration, and privacy protections, making it ideal for secure and seamless web browsing across Apple devices.

- **Mail**: The Mail app supports multiple accounts (including Gmail, Yahoo, and Exchange) and offers customizable features for managing emails and organizing mailboxes efficiently.

- **Calendar**: The Calendar app integrates with your Apple ID, allowing you to schedule events, set reminders, and sync calendars across devices for time management.

- **Photos**: The Photos app stores and organizes your photos and videos. It offers editing tools and iCloud Photo Library integration, so your media is backed up and accessible on all Apple devices.

- **Notes and Reminders**: These apps help with note-taking, task management, and reminders, all of which can sync via iCloud.

- **Other Notable Apps**: Apps like Messages, FaceTime, Maps, Preview, and Music cover communication, navigation, media, and productivity needs. For creative work, **GarageBand** (for music) and **iMovie** (for video editing) are included as well.

These pre-installed apps are optimized for macOS, offering high efficiency, seamless iCloud integration, and cross-device functionality.

2. Using the App Store to Download New Apps

The App Store is Apple's official platform for downloading a variety of macOS apps, ensuring they're safe and optimized for your system:

- **Accessing the App Store**:
  - Open the **App Store** from the Dock or Applications folder.
  - You'll find categories, curated collections, and personalized recommendations based on your activity.
- **Downloading and Updating Apps**:
  - Search for an app and click **Get** or **Download**. Free apps require only your Apple ID, while paid apps will require confirmation through a payment method.
  - **Automatic Updates**: Enable automatic updates by going to **System Settings > App Store** to keep your apps up to date without manual intervention.
- **Exploring Mac-Specific Apps**: Popular categories include productivity tools, creative software, games, and

educational resources tailored for macOS, with user reviews and ratings to guide your choices.

3. Installing and Managing Third-Party Software

While the App Store offers a curated selection, you may need to install third-party software for specialized needs. Here's how to install and manage it securely:

- **Downloading Third-Party Software**:
  - Download macOS-compatible software directly from the developer's website or reputable software distribution sites.
  - After downloading a **.dmg** (disk image) or **.pkg** file, open it to install the application. macOS may display a prompt to confirm the source; click **Open** and follow the on-screen instructions.

- **Managing App Permissions**:
  - For security, macOS uses **Gatekeeper** to block unauthorized apps. You can allow apps from identified developers under **System Settings > Privacy & Security**.
  - Customize app permissions for camera, microphone, location, and other features by going to **System Settings > Privacy & Security**.

- **Updating and Uninstalling Third-Party Apps**:
  - Most third-party apps include an **auto-update** feature or manual update option within the app settings.

- To uninstall, drag the app from **Applications** to **Trash**. Alternatively, use an uninstaller tool if provided, as some apps leave residual files.

Apple's Suite of Productivity Apps

Productivity apps like Pages, Keynote, and Numbers are designed for document creation, presentations, and spreadsheets. They offer seamless integration with macOS and iOS. Each app is optimized for the Apple ecosystem, with real-time collaboration, iCloud sync, and easy sharing options.

1. Pages (Word Processing)

Pages is Apple's word processor, comparable to Microsoft Word, tailored for creating documents, reports, and written content with a focus on design and ease of use.

- **Key Features**:
  - **Templates**: Pages offer a variety of templates for documents, including resumes, letters, brochures, and reports, which streamline the design process.
  - **Formatting Tools**: Users can add images, videos, and graphics, and style text with different fonts and colors. Pages also support **Smart Annotation** for easy markup.
  - **Collaboration**: Real-time collaboration is possible via iCloud. Team members can co-edit documents on their devices and see changes as they happen.

Pages combine simplicity with advanced design features, making them ideal for both professional and creative projects.

2. Keynote (Presentations)

Keynote is Apple's alternative to Microsoft PowerPoint, designed for creating dynamic, visually engaging presentations.

- **Key Features**:
    - **Animations and Transitions**: Keynote includes high-quality transitions and animations for text, images, and charts, enhancing presentation flow.
    - **Live Collaboration**: Like Pages, Keynote supports live collaboration, allowing multiple users to work on a presentation simultaneously.
    - **Remote Control**: With Keynote for iOS, users can control presentations on a MacBook from an iPhone or iPad, making it convenient for on-stage presentations.

Keynote's user-friendly interface and professional templates simplify the creation of polished presentations, ideal for business meetings, academic presentations, or creative showcases.

3. Numbers (Spreadsheets)

Numbers is Apple's spreadsheet app, offering a flexible and visually appealing alternative to Microsoft Excel.

- **Key Features**:
    - **Templates and Graphs**: Numbers provides templates for budgets, invoices, and more, and supports visually appealing charts and graphs that update with real-time data.

- ○ **Flexible Layouts**: Unlike the grid-centric layout of Excel, Numbers allows users to arrange tables, images, and text boxes freely on the canvas, enabling more visually dynamic spreadsheets.

- ○ **Collaborative Tools**: Real-time collaboration is available through iCloud, allowing teams to work on data analysis, budgeting, or planning together.

Numbers is particularly suitable for users who want a flexible and visually enhanced approach to spreadsheet management and data presentation.

Using the Productivity Suite Together

Apple's productivity suite is designed to work seamlessly together, enhancing cross-app functionality:

- **Sharing and Exporting**: Each app supports exporting to Microsoft-compatible formats, such as Word, Excel, and PowerPoint, making it easy to share with non-Apple users.

- **iCloud Integration**: All documents are saved to iCloud, enabling access across Apple devices. Changes made on one device sync instantly to others, which is convenient for on-the-go productivity.

- **Consistency in Design**: The unified design language across Pages, Keynote, and Numbers makes it easy to switch between apps, as the interfaces are consistent and intuitive.

Apple's productivity apps are ideal for MacBook Pro users looking for powerful, yet easy-to-use tools for creating documents, presentations, and spreadsheets that are visually compelling and well-suited for collaboration.

Optimizing M4 Pro/M4 Max hardware

Optimizing the hardware of the **M4 Pro and M4 Max MacBook Pro** with macOS Sequoia is essential if you want to unlock the full potential of this high-performance machine, especially for creative and professional tasks. Here's how macOS Sequoia's built-in features and app optimizations can leverage the advanced capabilities of the M4 Pro and Max chips to enhance productivity, speed, and efficiency:

---

1. Leveraging UMA for Creative Applications

The M4 Pro and M4 Max use a **Unified Memory Architecture** (UMA), which allows the CPU and GPU to share memory. This architecture minimizes data duplication and enables faster access to data, which is particularly beneficial for applications that demand high-speed memory access, such as video editing and 3D rendering.

Optimized Apps: Creative applications like Final Cut Pro, Logic Pro, Adobe Premiere Pro, and Blender are optimized to take advantage of the UMA in macOS. This optimization results in faster data processing, reduced load times, and smoother performance during intensive tasks like 4K and 8K video editing and complex audio production.

2. Maximizing M4 Chip Power with ProRes and ProRAW Support

The M4 Pro and M4 Max are equipped with dedicated ProRes and ProRAW accelerators. This hardware-specific support allows macOS to handle ProRes video editing in Final Cut Pro or DaVinci

Resolve much more efficiently, delivering real-time playback and faster export times.

macOS Integration: macOS Sequoia is optimized for ProRes and ProRAW, enabling native support in applications like Photos, Preview, and Finder. This feature allows professionals to preview and edit ProRAW photos and ProRes videos without needing to convert file formats, making workflows smoother and more efficient.

3. Enhanced Performance for Machine Learning and AI Tasks

The M4 Pro and Max's Neural Engines are designed to handle machine learning tasks with high efficiency, allowing for faster processing in AI-powered applications.

Core ML Integration: Apple's Core ML framework allows applications like Pixelmator Pro, Photoshop, and Final Cut Pro to leverage the Neural Engine for tasks such as image recognition, style transfer, and object removal. These machine learning tasks run up to twice as fast on M4 Max compared to previous models, saving creative professionals valuable time.

4. Maximizing Graphics with GPU-Intensive Tasks

The M4 Max features a significantly larger GPU with up to 40 cores, making it ideal for GPU-intensive tasks such as 3D modelling, CAD, and visual effects. Apps like Maya, Cinema 4D, and Adobe After Effects can utilize the full power of the M4 Max GPU for real-time rendering and high-resolution previews.

Metal API and macOS Optimization: macOS Sequoia includes an optimized Metal API, which supports efficient GPU rendering and acceleration. Creative software that relies on Metal, like Blender, can take full advantage of the M4 Max's GPU, resulting in smoother performance and faster render times.

5. Storage and File Management with High-Speed SSDs

The M4 series MacBook Pros are equipped with ultra-fast **NVMe SSDs**, which allow quick loading of large files, a vital feature for professionals working with high-resolution media files or extensive databases.

macOS File Management: macOS's Finder is optimized to quickly index and search through files on these high-speed SSDs, and features like Spotlight Search allow users to instantly locate files. This setup streamlines workflows by reducing the time needed to find and manage assets.

6. Energy Efficiency for Extended Work Sessions

macOS Sequoia is designed to optimize energy use based on the hardware demands of the M4 Pro and Max, resulting in extended battery life. For professionals on the go, this energy efficiency enables longer work sessions without the need to recharge frequently.

Power Modes: macOS also includes power modes, such as **Low Power Mode** for casual use and **High Power Mode** (exclusive to M4 Max) for intensive tasks. High Power Mode allocates more resources to demanding applications, ensuring that tasks like video rendering and 3D animation receive maximum performance.

7. iCloud and Seamless Cross-Device Integration

- **iCloud Drive and Continuity Features**: macOS Sequoia integrates deeply with iCloud, allowing professionals to store and access their projects from any Apple device. Features like **Handoff**, **Universal Clipboard**, and **AirDrop** make it easy to move files and data across devices, supporting smooth workflows and reducing downtime.

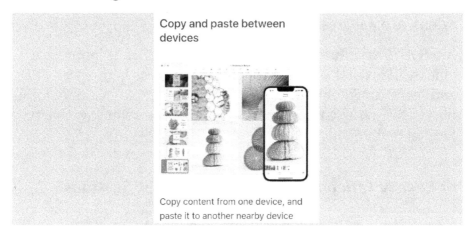

Copy and paste between devices

Copy content from one device, and paste it to another nearby device

The combination of the M4 Pro and M4 Max's cutting-edge hardware with macOS Sequoia's software optimizations creates a powerful environment for creative professionals. By leveraging these features, you can enhance performance in graphics, rendering, machine learning, and productivity.

CONNECTIVITY AND PERIPHERALS

The MacBook Pro M4 series is designed to provide seamless connectivity options and support for a variety of peripherals, making it ideal for professional and personal use. This is how to set up and optimize connectivity and peripherals on your MacBook Pro.

Connecting to Wi-Fi, Bluetooth, and Other Networks

Wi-Fi Setup and Management:

- o **Connecting to Wi-Fi**: To connect to a Wi-Fi network, go to **System Settings > Wi-Fi** in macOS, where you can choose from available networks. For secure networks, you'll be prompted to enter a password.

- o **Optimized Performance**: The M4 Pro/Max includes advanced wireless networking features to improve Wi-Fi stability, speed, and security. Features like **Wi-Fi 6E** support ensure faster speeds and lower latency for streaming, downloading large files, or remote work.

- o **Troubleshooting**: If you encounter issues, macOS provides diagnostics tools under **System Settings > Network**, which helps identify and resolve common Wi-Fi connectivity issues.

Bluetooth Connectivity:

- o **Pairing Bluetooth Devices**: Navigate to **System Settings > Bluetooth** to pair devices like headphones, mice, keyboards, or speakers. The MacBook Pro will automatically search for nearby Bluetooth devices, allowing for quick pairing.

- o **Advanced Bluetooth 5.3**: The latest version of Bluetooth allows for improved audio quality, faster connection speeds, and better power efficiency.

- o **Troubleshooting Bluetooth**: If you experience connectivity issues, you can reset Bluetooth preferences in System Settings. For more advanced fixes, use macOS diagnostics or reset the Bluetooth module from the terminal.

Connecting to Ethernet (with Adapter):

- o **Using Ethernet**: For a wired connection, you'll need a USB-C to Ethernet adapter, which can be connected to any Thunderbolt/USB-C port on your MacBook. Ethernet provides a reliable, high-speed connection, ideal for large file transfers or streaming high-definition content.

Using External Displays and Configuring Display Settings

1. **Connecting External Displays**:

Supported Resolutions and Configurations: The M4 Pro and M4 Max support multiple external displays with high resolutions. The M4 Pro supports up to two 6K displays, while the M4 Max can handle up to three 6K displays and one 4K display.

Using Thunderbolt Ports: To connect external displays, use Thunderbolt 4 ports, or Thunderbolt 5 depending on your model, which support high-resolution monitors. Adapters like Thunderbolt to HDMI or Thunderbolt to DisplayPort may be required depending on the monitor's input options.

2. **Configuring Display Settings**:

Adjusting Display Arrangements: In **System Settings > Displays**, you can manage display arrangements, resolutions, and other preferences. You can choose **Extended Mode** for multi-screen setups or **Mirror Mode** to display the same content across monitors.

Advanced Settings: For creative professionals, you can enable **HDR** and fine-tune colour profiles under the Display settings, allowing for accurate colour representation—essential for video editing, design, and photography.

ProMotion and Refresh Rate: The built-in display supports **ProMotion** with up to a 120Hz refresh rate, and compatible external monitors can also be set to match these refresh rates in **System Settings > Displays**.

3. **Apple's Sidecar and AirPlay**:

Sidecar: You can use an iPad as an additional display by selecting **Sidecar** in **System Settings**. Sidecar offers a wireless, low-latency solution that's especially useful for drawing, note-taking, or as a secondary screen.

AirPlay to Mac: With **AirPlay**, you can wirelessly mirror or extend the screen to compatible Apple devices. This feature is handy for presentations, watching content on a larger screen, or extending your workspace.

Connecting and Using Peripherals

The MacBook Pro M4 series provides extensive compatibility with various peripherals, including printers, external drives, and audio devices. Below is a guide on how to connect and utilize these peripherals effectively.

1. Connecting Printers

- **Wireless Printers**: To connect a wireless printer, ensure it's on the same Wi-Fi network as your MacBook. Go to **System Settings > Printers & Scanners**. Click the "+"

button to add a new printer. Your Mac will search for available printers; select your printer from the list and follow the prompts to install any necessary drivers automatically.

- **USB Printers**: For USB printers, connect the printer directly to the MacBook using a USB-C cable. Your Mac should automatically recognize the printer. If it doesn't, follow the same steps as for wireless printers.

- **AirPrint**: Many modern printers support AirPrint, allowing you to print from your Mac without additional drivers. Simply select the AirPrint-enabled printer when printing documents.

2. Connecting External Drives

- **Using Thunderbolt and USB-C**: The MacBook Pro M4 series features Thunderbolt 4 and USB-C ports, allowing for high-speed connections with external drives. Simply connect your external hard drive or SSD to one of the available ports. The drive should appear on your desktop or in the Finder sidebar.

- **Format Compatibility**: Ensure that the external drive is formatted in a compatible file system (APFS, Mac OS Extended, or exFAT for cross-compatibility with Windows). If necessary, use **Disk Utility** (found in **Applications > Utilities**) to format the drive before use.

- **Managing Storage**: Use Finder to organize files on your external drive. You can create folders, move files, and manage data as needed. External drives are great for backups, large file storage, or transferring data between devices.

- **Bluetooth Audio Devices**: To connect Bluetooth headphones, speakers, or microphones, go to **System Settings > Bluetooth**. Make sure your audio device is in pairing mode and select it from the list to connect.

- **Wired Audio Devices**: For wired connections, use the headphone jack or USB-C port. If your audio device uses a 3.5mm jack, simply plug it into the headphone port. For USB-C devices, connect using a compatible USB-C audio adapter if necessary.

- **Sound Settings**: Adjust your audio output settings by going to **System Settings > Sound**. Here, you can choose your preferred output device and adjust volume levels.

AirDrop, Handoff, and Continuity Camera

The MacBook Pro M4 series, with its integration into Apple's ecosystem, supports features like **AirDrop**, **Handoff**, and **Continuity Camera**. These functions enable seamless sharing and productivity across Apple devices, enhancing user experience and convenience.

1. AirDrop

AirDrop allows you to wirelessly share files, photos, and other content with nearby Apple devices over Wi-Fi and Bluetooth. It's particularly useful for transferring large files quickly between devices without needing cables or the internet.

- **How to Use AirDrop**:
  - On your MacBook, open **Finder**, go to **AirDrop** in the sidebar and make sure AirDrop is enabled.

- To share a file, right-click it, select **Share > AirDrop**, and choose a nearby device.

move your pointer over the password to reveal it. You can also edit or delete as password, or click 📤 to share it with AirDrop.

- Ensure the receiving device has AirDrop enabled and is set to accept transfers from contacts or everyone.

- **Benefits**: AirDrop is fast, secure (using encryption), and highly efficient for transferring files, especially between macOS and iOS devices. This feature saves time and effort, especially in collaborative or creative environments where file-sharing is frequent.

2. Handoff

Handoff lets you start a task on one Apple device and continue it on another. For example, you can start writing an email on your iPhone and pick up exactly where you left off on your MacBook. Handoff works with apps like Mail, Safari, Notes, Messages, and more.

- **How to Use Handoff**:

- To enable Handoff, go to **System Settings > General > AirDrop & Handoff** on your MacBook and ensure **Handoff** is toggled on.

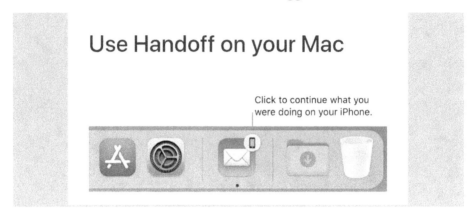

- When using a compatible app on one device, the app icon will appear in the **Dock** on your MacBook or as a suggestion on other Apple devices.

Handoff streamlines your workflow, allowing you to effortlessly switch between devices. This is especially helpful for multi-taskers and users who frequently alternate between devices for different tasks.

3. Continuity Camera

Continuity Camera lets you use your iPhone as a high-quality webcam or scan documents directly into your MacBook. This feature is perfect for video calls, content creation, and document management.

- **How to Use Continuity Camera**:
  - To use your iPhone as a webcam, ensure both devices are signed in to the same Apple ID and are on the same Wi-Fi network.

- For scanning, open an app on your MacBook that supports Continuity Camera, such as **Notes** or **Finder**. Right-click and choose **Import from iPhone > Scan Documents** or **Take Photo**. The iPhone will activate the camera, allowing you to scan directly.

Benefits: Continuity Camera enhances video quality for calls and content, making it ideal for remote work and creative tasks. The document scanning feature streamlines digitizing paperwork, which is valuable for both personal and professional organizations.

USING SAFARI AND WEB BROWSING FEATURES

Safari, Apple's default browser, offers an array of features designed to enhance browsing efficiency, privacy, and integration across Apple devices. Here's a guide to setting up and using Safari on your MacBook Pro M4.

Setting Up Safari and Managing Bookmarks

1. **Initial Setup**: When you open Safari for the first time, you can customize the start page by adding favourites, frequently visited sites, and suggested websites. This setup provides quick access to the sites you use the most.

2. **Managing Bookmarks**:

   o To save a site as a bookmark, go to **Bookmarks > Add Bookmark** or use the shortcut Command + D.

   o Organize your bookmarks by creating folders in **Bookmarks > Edit Bookmarks**.

   o Use the **favourites Bar** to keep frequently accessed sites one click away.

This organized bookmark structure improves productivity by making it easy to locate and revisit key websites.

Using Privacy Features and Settings in Safari

Safari is designed with robust privacy features to protect user data and enhance secure browsing:

1. **Intelligent Tracking Prevention (ITP)**: ITP automatically blocks third-party trackers, preventing advertisers from following you across the web.

2. **Privacy Report**: Safari's Privacy Report provides a summary of all trackers blocked over the last 30 days, accessible by clicking the **shield icon** next to the URL bar. This gives you insight into which sites are trying to track your data.

3. **Private Browsing Mode**:
   - To open a private browsing window, go to **File > New Private Window** or use the shortcut Command + Shift + N. In this mode, Safari won't save your browsing history, cookies, or autofill information.

4. **Security Settings**:
   - Adjust privacy preferences in **Safari > Settings > Privacy** to control cookies, website data, and whether sites can request location access.

These privacy settings allow you to navigate the web securely, minimizing the data collected from your online activity.

Safari's Tab Management and Browsing History

1. **Tab Groups**: Safari's **Tab Groups** feature allows you to organize tabs for different tasks or projects. To create a Tab Group, click on the **Sidebar** (or Shift + Command + L), select **New Tab Group**, and add tabs related to that topic.

2. **Pinned Tabs**: Pin frequently used websites by right-clicking the tab and selecting **Pin Tab**. Pinned tabs stay open and are accessible across all windows.

3. **Browsing History**:

   o Access your browsing history by selecting **History** in the menu bar, where you can revisit sites and manage saved pages.

   o You can also clear your history selectively or entirely by going to **History > Clear History**.

Tab management tools help streamline navigation and improve productivity by organizing frequently visited sites and providing efficient access to past web activity.

Syncing Bookmarks and Data Across Devices with iCloud

Safari leverages iCloud to sync your bookmarks, history, and reading lists across all Apple devices logged into the same iCloud account. Here's how to set up syncing:

1. **Enable iCloud for Safari**:

   o Open **System Settings > Apple ID > iCloud** and ensure that Safari syncing is enabled.

2. **Benefits**:

   o Your bookmarks, reading list, and open tabs automatically sync across your Mac, iPhone, iPad, and other Apple devices. This feature enables seamless transitions between devices, allowing you to pick up browsing exactly where you left off.

Using iCloud sync is ideal for anyone frequently switching between devices, as it keeps all browsing data accessible across platforms.

MANAGING BATTERY AND POWER EFFICIENCY

The MacBook Pro M4 series models are equipped with Apple's advanced energy-efficient technology, but managing battery life can enhance both performance and device longevity.

Battery Care Tips

1. **Avoid Extreme Temperatures**: The optimal temperature range for a MacBook is between 50°F and 95°F (10°C to 35°C). Avoid using the MacBook in very hot or cold environments, as extreme temperatures can degrade battery capacity over time.

2. **Partial Charging and Discharging**: Frequently charging between 20% and 80% rather than letting the battery drain fully or charging to 100% can prolong battery life.

3. **Update Software Regularly**: Apple often releases software updates that include optimizations for battery life. Ensure that your macOS is up to date to benefit from these improvements.

These simple care habits can have a significant impact on maintaining battery health and ensuring long-term efficiency.

Optimizing Battery Life through Settings

1. **Adjust Display Brightness**: Lowering the screen brightness is one of the easiest ways to reduce power consumption. You can adjust this by pressing the brightness keys on the keyboard or in **System Settings > Displays**.

2. **Enable Battery Saver Mode**: Under **System Settings > Battery**, select **Low Power Mode**. This setting reduces background activity and lowers power usage by limiting processing power when the MacBook is unplugged.

3. **Sleep Settings**: Adjust sleep settings to put your MacBook to sleep more quickly when idle. In **System Settings > Battery**, you can control how long the MacBook stays awake when on battery power or plugged in.

Managing Background Apps

1. **Quit Unused Applications**: Keep only necessary apps running. To see what's active, check the **Activity Monitor** in **Applications > Utilities**. Here, you can quit apps that are consuming significant power.

2. **Reduce Startup Programs**: Minimize startup programs that automatically launch when you start your MacBook by going to **System Settings > General > Login Items**. Removing unnecessary startup items reduces background processing, enhancing both power efficiency and performance.

3. **Close Background Browser Tabs**: Safari and other browsers use substantial power, especially with multiple tabs open. Closing unnecessary tabs or switching to a more energy-efficient browser mode can help conserve battery life.

Battery Health Monitoring

1. **Check Battery Health Status**:

Go to **System Settings > Battery** and click **Battery Health**. Here, you can view the maximum capacity percentage and confirm whether the battery is in **Normal** or **Service Recommended** status.

2. **Enable Optimized Battery Charging**: This feature learns your charging routine and delays charging past 80% until it's needed, reducing wear. Enable it in **System Settings > Battery > Battery Health**.

3. **Monitor with Activity Monitor**: In **Activity Monitor**, click the **Energy** tab to see which applications are consuming the most power. This can be useful for identifying apps that are draining the battery unusually fast.

Battery health monitoring allows you to keep track of battery performance over time and ensure efficient power usage for both short and long-term use.

How to use macOS Power-Saving Options and Low Power Mode

The macOS sequoia is optimized with different power-saving features to extend battery life and reduce energy consumption. Here's how to leverage these tools.

Low Power Mode

Low Power Mode is designed to conserve battery by reducing the MacBook's power usage when unplugged. When activated, it limits background activity, reduces screen brightness, lowers processor speed, and modifies system animations.

To Enable Low Power Mode:

Go to **System Settings > Battery** and select **Low Power Mode**. You can choose to turn it on **always**, **when on battery power**, or **never**.

Low Power Mode is especially beneficial when you're away from a power source and need to extend battery life, such as during travel or long workdays.

Other Power-Saving Options in macOS

1. **Automatic Brightness and Screen Off**:
   - Lowering display brightness saves significant power. You can also enable **Automatic Brightness** in **System Settings > Displays** to adjust brightness based on ambient light.

- o Adjust **the Turn display off after** settings in **System Settings > Battery** to automatically put the screen to sleep when idle.

2. **Energy Saver Options**:

   - o In **System Settings > Battery**, choose **Battery** or **Power Adapter** settings to adjust sleep timing for both battery and plugged-in states.

   - o By setting the **Prevent your Mac from automatically sleeping when the display is off** option to off, you allow the MacBook to go to sleep and save power when not in use.

3. **App Nap and Background App Refresh**:

   - o macOS uses **App Nap** to pause background apps when they're hidden or minimized, conserving battery. There's no setting to turn this on or off as it's automatic, but closing unnecessary apps and tabs can help App Nap work more effectively.

   - o **Background App Refresh** controls what apps can update in the background, which helps conserve power when on battery. Go to **System Settings > General > Background App Refresh** to turn off updates for specific apps.

Tips for Effective Use of Power-Saving Settings

- **Use Dark Mode**: In **System Settings > Appearance**, select **Dark Mode** to reduce power usage by minimizing screen brightness.

Choose the color scheme for your Mac.

Click an item in the sidebar to adjust settings.

- **Manage Startup and Login Items**: Limit startup programs by going to **System Settings > General > Login Items**. Fewer login items reduce CPU demand, especially during startup.

- **Battery Health Management**: Enable **Optimized Battery Charging** in **System Settings > Battery > Battery Health** to reduce the battery's charging load, prolonging its lifespan by minimizing full-charge cycles.

ADVANCED FEATURES AND PRO

The MacBook Pro M4 series is packed with powerful features and tools to improve productivity and streamline workflows when you leverage features like the Touch Bar, trackpad gestures, multitasking capabilities, and optimizing professional software.

Touch Bar Settings and Shortcuts

The MacBook Pro's Touch Bar adapts to different apps, offering shortcuts that improve speed and ease of access. You can customize the Touch Bar to suit your workflow:

1. **Customizing the Touch Bar**:

   o Go to **System Settings > Keyboard** and select **Customize Touch Bar**. Drag items to the Touch Bar to add shortcuts for volume, brightness, screenshots, or other frequently used functions.

2. **App-Specific Controls**: Many apps, like Safari and Photos, display unique Touch Bar controls. For instance, in Safari, you'll see quick navigation buttons for bookmarks, tabs, and searches.

3. **Using Function Keys**:

   o Press the **Fn key** or **Globe key** to display the function keys on the Touch Bar when needed, such as for software that requires F1-F12 keys.

Personalizing the Touch Bar lets you quickly access key functions in your favourite apps, saving time and reducing the need to navigate menus.

Customizing Trackpad Gestures for Productivity

The large, responsive trackpad on the MacBook Pro M4 series supports a variety of gestures that streamline navigation and multitasking. You can customize these gestures in **System Settings > Trackpad**:

1. **Key Productivity Gestures**:

    o **Swipe between apps**: Use a three-finger swipe left or right to switch between open applications quickly.

    o **App Exposé**: Swipe down with three fingers to see all open windows of the current app.

    o **Mission Control**: Swipe up with three fingers to access Mission Control and view all open windows.

2. **Customizing Gestures**:

    o Under **System Settings > Trackpad**, you can adjust the sensitivity and customize gestures, such as changing three-finger swipes to four-finger gestures.

Mastering trackpad gestures allows for fluid multitasking, making it faster to switch between tasks and applications without relying on the keyboard.

Using Split View and Multitasking Efficiently

macOS Sequoia's multitasking features, like Split View, make it easy to work in multiple applications side-by-side:

1. **Split View**:

- In any open app window, click and hold the green **full-screen button** in the top-left corner, then select **Tile Window to Left of Screen** or **Tile Window to Right of Screen**.

- Choose another app to fill the other half of the screen, making it easy to reference information or multitask without switching windows.

2. **Using Mission Control**:

- Use Mission Control (F3 key or swipe up with three fingers) to see all open apps and desktops, making it easy to organize your workspace and drag windows to different virtual desktops.

Split View and Mission Control enhance multitasking by allowing you to keep relevant apps and windows side-by-side, ideal for workflows that require referencing multiple sources or applications.

Tips for Professional Software Usage

The M4 Pro and M4 Max models, with their powerful GPUs and high RAM capacities, are optimized for intensive creative applications. Here's how to get the most out of software like Final Cut Pro and Logic Pro:

1. **Final Cut Pro**:

- **Optimize Media**: Use **Optimized and Proxy Media** settings to reduce processing demand when editing high-resolution video. This setting is accessible in **File > Import** options.

- **Background Rendering**: Final Cut Pro allows background rendering for smoother playback.

Adjust settings in **Preferences > Playback** for optimal performance.

- ○ **Keyboard Shortcuts**: Customize keyboard shortcuts for editing tools like blade, trim, and insert to speed up the editing process.

2. **Logic Pro**:

- ○ **Track Stacks**: Use Track Stacks to organize and simplify complex projects with multiple layers. Access Track Stacks through **Track > Create Track Stack**.

- ○ **Smart Controls**: Map hardware controls to Smart Controls in Logic Pro to adjust effects, EQ, and other parameters without opening multiple plugins.

- ○ **Low Latency Mode**: Enable Low Latency Mode in **Preferences > Audio** to reduce delay during live recording.

SECURITY AND PRIVACY

Like every other Apple MacBook Pro, the Pro M4 series offers robust security and privacy features to protect your data, device, and personal information. Here's how to set up security features like Touch ID, Find My Mac, and FileVault, and how to manage privacy settings for enhanced protection.

Setting up Touch ID and Face ID

1. **Touch ID**:

   - The MacBook Pro M4 comes with an embedded **Touch ID sensor** in the top-right corner of the keyboard for secure unlocking and authorizing actions.

   - To set it up, go to **System Settings > Touch ID & Password**. Follow the prompts to scan your fingerprint, which can be used to unlock your device, authorize purchases, and sign into apps securely.

2. **Face ID**:

   - While not available on every model, Face ID (if present) provides secure facial recognition to unlock the device and approve purchases.

   - Setup is under **System Settings > Face ID & Password**. Follow the prompts to scan your face, ensuring a reliable, quick unlock and authentication experience.

Enabling Find My Mac for Security

Find My Mac helps locate your device if it's ever lost or stolen. It enables you to track, lock, or remotely erase your MacBook from another Apple device.

- To enable it, go to **System Settings > Apple ID > iCloud > Find My Mac** and switch it on. You'll need to allow location access for this feature to work effectively.

- If your MacBook is lost, you can use the **Find My app** on any iOS device or via iCloud.com to locate or secure your device remotely.

Configuring Privacy Settings for Location, Microphone, and Camera

To control which apps have access to your personal data, macOS offers fine-tuned privacy controls:

1. **Location Services**:

Go to **System Settings > Privacy & Security > Location Services**. Here, you can toggle location access on or off for individual apps, ensuring only trusted applications use your location.

2. **Microphone and Camera Access**:

In **System Settings > Privacy & Security**, choose **Microphone** and **Camera** settings. Toggle access for each app based on your preference. Only allow permissions for apps you trust, which helps prevent unauthorized access to these features.

3. **App Permissions**:

Within **Privacy & Security**, you can adjust permissions for other data, like Photos, Contacts, and Screen Recording, offering you full control over which apps can access sensitive data.

Using FileVault to Encrypt Data

FileVault is Apple's encryption feature that secures your entire hard drive, protecting your files even if the MacBook is lost or stolen.

- Enable it by going to **System Settings > Privacy & Security > FileVault** and following the prompts. You'll be asked to set a recovery key and password, so be sure to store these securely as they are essential for accessing your encrypted data.

- Once enabled, FileVault encrypts all data on your disk, requiring your password or Touch ID for access. This encryption helps prevent unauthorized access to your data.

Secure Access to Files and Accounts

To protect specific files and accounts, macOS includes additional features:

1. **Secure Password Management**:

    o Use **iCloud Keychain** to securely store and autofill passwords across Apple devices. You can manage saved passwords in **System Settings > Passwords**.

    o iCloud Keychain generates strong, unique passwords for you, reducing the risk of compromised accounts.

2. **Screen Lock Settings**:

- Set a short lock screen timer to automatically lock your MacBook when idle. Adjust this in **System Settings > Lock Screen** for increased security.

3. **Guest User Accounts**:

- Enable **Guest User accounts** for others who need temporary access, ensuring they can't access your files. Go to **System Settings > Users & Groups** to enable and manage guest accounts.

By setting up these security and privacy features, you can ensure a safer experience.

TROUBLESHOOTING COMMON ISSUES

The MacBook Pro M4 is generally reliable, but like any device, occasional issues can arise. Here's what you need to do to solve some common problems.

Wi-Fi and Network Connectivity Issues

1. **Check Wi-Fi Settings**:

   o Make sure Wi-Fi is enabled in **System Settings > Network**. If you're experiencing slow or unstable connections, try toggling Wi-Fi off and on or restarting your router.

2. **Forget and Rejoin Network**:

   o Sometimes, rejoining the network can resolve connectivity issues. Go to **System Settings > Wi-Fi**, select the network, and choose "Forget this Network." Reconnect by entering your password.

3. **Update macOS**:

   o Network issues can often be resolved by installing macOS updates that include connectivity fixes. Go to **System Settings > Software Update** and install any available updates.

4. **Reset Network Settings**:

   o If issues persist, you may need to reset network settings. Use **System Settings > Network** to create a new network profile, which may resolve conflicts or corrupt settings.

Battery Performance and Power Management Problems

1. **Optimizing Battery Settings**:

   o Battery drain may result from resource-heavy apps or background tasks. Go to **System Settings > Battery** and enable **Optimized Battery Charging** and **Low Power Mode** to extend battery life.

2. **Identify Battery Drainers**:

   o Use **Activity Monitor** (found in **Applications > Utilities**) to check which apps are consuming the most power. Close or limit high-usage apps to conserve battery.

3. **Calibrate Battery**:

   o Occasionally letting the battery fully discharge, then charging it to 100%, can help recalibrate battery health indicators.

4. **Battery Replacement**:

   o If battery life is significantly reduced over time, the battery may need replacement. Check battery health in **System Settings > Battery > Battery Health** and contact Apple Support if necessary.

MacBook Freezing or Slowing Down

1. **Restart the MacBook**:

   o Often, a simple restart can clear temporary system issues. Select **Apple Menu > Restart** to refresh the system.

2. **Clear System Storage**:

   o Over time, files and cached data can slow down the MacBook. Go to **System Settings > Storage** to view usage and delete unnecessary files or cache.

3. **Manage Startup Programs**:

   o Too many startup apps can cause slowdowns. Go to **System Settings > General > Login Items** and remove any unnecessary items.

4. **Run First Aid in Disk Utility**:

   o Use **Disk Utility** (found in **Applications > Utilities**) to run **First Aid**, which checks and repairs disk issues that could be causing slowdowns.

Restarting, Resetting, and Recovering the System

1. **Force Restart**:

   o If the MacBook is unresponsive, hold down the **Power button** until it shuts off, then press it again to restart.

2. **Reset NVRAM/PRAM**:

   o For persistent issues like display or audio problems, reset the NVRAM/PRAM by restarting and holding **the Option + Command + P + R** keys until the system reboots.

3. **Entering Recovery Mode**:

   o If serious issues prevent macOS from loading, enter **Recovery Mode** by holding **Command + R** during startup. In Recovery Mode, you can reinstall macOS, use Disk Utility, or restore from a backup.

4. **Reinstall macOS**:

   o If issues persist, reinstalling macOS can resolve software-related problems. In Recovery Mode, choose **Reinstall macOS** and follow the prompts.

Accessing Apple Support and Troubleshooting Resources

1. **Apple Support Website**:

   o Visit Apple Support for guides, articles, and live support options for specific issues.

2. **Apple Support App**:

   o Download the **Apple Support App** on an iPhone or iPad to get personalized support, chat with a representative, or schedule an appointment at an Apple Store.

3. **Apple Diagnostics**:

   o Run **Apple Diagnostics** by holding down the **D key** during startup to identify hardware issues. This diagnostic tool can help determine if there's a hardware component that may need repair.

BACKUP AND DATA MANAGEMENT

Data protection and recovery are essential parts of MacBook usage, especially for high-value work.

Using Time Machine for Regular Backups

Time Machine is Apple's built-in solution for backing up your data to an external drive. It automatically saves copies of your files and keeps track of changes so you can restore previous versions.

1. **Set Up Time Machine**:

   o   Connect an external hard drive to your MacBook and go to **System Settings > Time Machine**.

   o   Choose the connected drive as the backup disk, and Time Machine will start creating regular backups.

2. **Automatic Backups**:

   o   Time Machine runs automatically, creating hourly, daily, and weekly backups without user intervention, which means your data stays safe without requiring constant management.

3. **Restoring Files from Time Machine**:

   o   To recover a file, open **Time Machine** from the **Dock** or **System Settings** and navigate through your backup history to the file version you want to restore.

iCloud Backups and Synchronization Across Apple Devices

iCloud offers cloud-based backup and sync options, allowing you to keep data up to date across all your Apple devices.

1. **Enable iCloud Sync**:

   o In **System Settings > Apple ID > iCloud**, you can select the data types you want to sync, such as Photos, Documents, and Contacts.

2. **Using iCloud Drive for File Backup**:

   o iCloud Drive automatically saves files stored in your **Desktop** and **Documents** folders, making it accessible across Apple devices.

- o By enabling **iCloud Drive**, you also gain the benefit of being able to access your files from any device logged into your Apple ID.

3. **iCloud Storage Management**:

   - o iCloud's free tier includes 5GB of storage, with additional paid options available. You can manage your storage under **System Settings > Apple ID > iCloud > Manage Storage** to optimize space and avoid hitting storage limits.

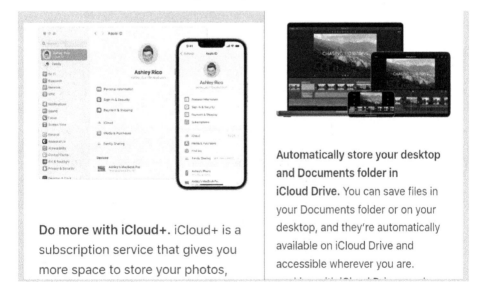

Do more with iCloud+. iCloud+ is a subscription service that gives you more space to store your photos,

Automatically store your desktop and Documents folder in iCloud Drive. You can save files in your Documents folder or on your desktop, and they're automatically available on iCloud Drive and accessible wherever you are.

External Backup Options and Best Practices

For added security, you may also want to use an external backup in addition to Time Machine and iCloud.

1. **Choosing an External Drive**:

High-capacity and reliable drives, like SSDs or high-quality HDDs, are recommended for external backups. Make sure the drive is formatted to work with macOS (APFS or HFS+ formats).

2. **Manual Backup**:

Manually copy and paste critical files or folders to an external drive periodically. This provides an additional layer of security against accidental data loss.

3. **Automated Backup Software**:

Consider using third-party tools like **Carbon Copy Cloner** or **SuperDuper!** for creating clones of your MacBook's hard drive, which can be booted in case of a critical failure.

Restoring from Backup and System Recovery

If you need to restore your MacBook, you can do so from a Time Machine or iCloud backup.

1. **Restoring from Time Machine**:

    o In case of data loss or a new system setup, use **macOS Recovery Mode**. Restart your MacBook, press **Command + R** until the Apple logo appears, and select **Restore from Time Machine**.

2. **Restoring iCloud Data**:

- o iCloud backups sync automatically; simply log in with your Apple ID on a new device, and your synced files, contacts, photos, and other data will be restored from iCloud.

3. **System Recovery from External Clone**:

- o If you've created a bootable clone of your system, you can use it to recover your MacBook by connecting the external drive and holding the **Option** on startup, then selecting the clone as the startup disk.

UPDATES AND MAINTENANCE

Keeping your MacBook Pro M4 in optimal condition involves regular updates, maintenance routines, and cleaning practices.

Keeping macOS and Apps Updated

1. **Regular macOS Updates**:

   o Apple frequently releases updates to enhance security, and performance, and add new features. To check for updates, go to **System Settings > Software Update**. It's advisable to enable **Automatic Updates** to receive updates as soon as they are available.

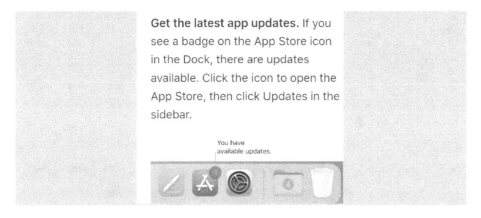

Get the latest app updates. If you see a badge on the App Store icon in the Dock, there are updates available. Click the icon to open the App Store, then click Updates in the sidebar.

You have available updates.

2. **Updating Applications**:

   o Regularly update your apps through the **App Store**. Go to **App Store > Updates** to see if any applications need updating. Keeping apps updated ensures compatibility with the latest macOS features and enhances overall stability.

3. **Benefits of Updating**:

- Updates can fix bugs, improve performance, and protect your MacBook from vulnerabilities. Many users neglect updates, but staying current is crucial for both security and performance.

4. **Disk Cleanup**:

  - Use **Storage Management** tools found in **System Settings > General > Storage** to identify large files and applications that you may not need. Regularly clearing out old files can free up valuable disk space and improve system performance.

5. **Manage Login Items**:

  - Reduce startup time by managing login items. Go to **System Settings > General > Login Items** and remove unnecessary applications that launch at startup.

6. **Monitor Activity**:

  - Use **Activity Monitor** (found in **Applications > Utilities**) to check for resource-hungry apps and processes. If you find an application consuming excessive CPU or memory, consider quitting or uninstalling it.

7. **Run First Aid**:

  - Regularly use **Disk Utility** to run First Aid on your drives, which checks for disk errors and repairs them

External Cleaning: For the exterior, use a soft, lint-free cloth slightly dampened with water or a mild cleaner. Avoid using harsh chemicals or aerosol sprays directly on the device. For the keyboard, you can use compressed air to blow out debris.

Display Care: Clean microfibre cloth to avoid scratches. If needed, slightly dampen the cloth with water or a screen-safe cleaner. Ensure the device is turned off before cleaning the screen.

Regular Cleaning Schedule: Aim to clean your MacBook Pro regularly (at least once a month) to maintain hygiene and prevent the buildup of dirt and grime that can affect performance and aesthetics.

Checking for Firmware Updates

Firmware updates can significantly enhance system stability and performance by improving hardware compatibility. These updates are often included with macOS updates but can also be specific to certain devices.

How to Check for Firmware Updates: To check if firmware updates are needed, simply perform a macOS update check. If any firmware updates are required, they will typically be included with the system updates.

Shortcuts and Commands Keyboard Shortcuts

This serves as a handy reference for keyboard shortcuts, trackpad gestures, and troubleshooting commands.

Keyboard Shortcuts for macOS and Commonly Used Apps

1. **General macOS Shortcuts**:
   - **Command (⌘) + C**: Copy
   - **Command (⌘) + V**: Paste
   - **Command (⌘) + X**: Cut
   - **Command (⌘) + Z**: Undo
   - **Command (⌘) + A**: Select All
   - **Command (⌘) + F**: Find

2. **Finder Shortcuts**:
   - **Command (⌘) + N**: Open a new Finder window
   - **Command (⌘) + Shift + N**: Create a new folder
   - **Command (⌘) + I**: Get Info on the selected item
   - **Command (⌘) + Delete**: Move selected item to Trash

3. **Safari Shortcuts**:
   - **Command (⌘) + T**: Open a new tab
   - **Command (⌘) + Shift + T**: Reopen the last closed tab

- o **Command (⌘) + L**: Highlight the URL bar

4. **Common App Shortcuts**:

   - o **Command (⌘) + P**: Print the current document
   - o **Command (⌘) + S**: Save the current document

Trackpad Gestures Reference

1. **Basic Gestures**:

   - o **Click**: Tap the trackpad once.
   - o **Secondary Click**: Tap with two fingers or click in the bottom right corner.
   - o **Scroll**: Slide two fingers up or down.

2. **Advanced Gestures**:

   - o **Zoom**: Pinch with two fingers.
   - o **Swipe between pages**: Swipe left or right with two fingers.
   - o **Mission Control**: Swipe up with three fingers or four fingers (depending on settings).
   - o **App Exposé**: Swipe down with three fingers to view all open windows for the current app.

3. **Customizing Gestures**:

   - o Go to **System Settings > Trackpad** to customize gestures according to your preference.

List of Troubleshooting Commands in Terminal for Advanced Users

1. **Basic Commands**:

   - **ping [hostname]**: Check network connectivity to a specific server.

   - **traceroute [hostname]**: Trace the route packets take to a network host.

   - **sudo shutdown -h now**: Shut down the Mac immediately (requires admin password).

2. **Disk Management**:

   - **diskutil list**: List all connected disks and partitions.

   - **fsck**: Filesystem consistency check (run in Recovery Mode).

3. **System Information**:

   - **system_profiler**: Displays detailed system information.

   - **top**: Display active processes and their resource usage in real time.

4. **Network Commands**:

   - **ifconfig**: Display or configure network interfaces.

   - **netstat -nr**: Show the routing table.

5. **File and Process Management**:

   - **killall [process name]**: Force quit an application by name.

   - **rm -rf [directory]**: Remove files or directories forcefully (use with caution).

By familiarizing yourself with these shortcuts and commands, you can navigate your MacBook Pro more efficiently and troubleshoot issues with greater ease.

WARRANTY AND SUPPORT

As an owner of a MacBook Pro M4 series, understanding the warranty, support options, and resources available to you is essential for maintaining your device and addressing any issues that may arise.

Understanding the Warranty for MacBook Pro

1. **Standard Warranty**:

   o Apple provides a one-year limited warranty that covers manufacturing defects and hardware failures. This includes coverage for the MacBook Pro itself and accessories, such as the power adapter. However, it does not cover accidental damage or misuse.

   o For extended coverage, you can purchase AppleCare+, which extends your warranty to three years from the original purchase date. AppleCare+ also includes up to two incidents of accidental damage protection (subject to a service fee), making it a wise investment for users prone to mishaps.

2. Eligibility for warranty service- your MacBook must be within the warranty period and must not have been damaged due to unauthorized modifications or misuse. You can check your warranty status by entering your device's serial number on the Apple Support website.

How to Access AppleCare+

- AppleCare+ can be purchased within 60 days of buying your MacBook Pro. You can do this online, at an Apple Store, or through authorized resellers.

2. **Claiming AppleCare+ Benefits**:
   - You can initiate a claim through the Apple Support app or by visiting the Apple Support website. You'll need to provide your device's serial number and may be prompted to arrange for shipping or bring your device to a local Apple Store.

Contacting Apple Support and Accessing Online.

For direct assistance, you can contact Apple Support through various channels:

   - **Phone**: Reach out to Apple Support via the phone number for your region.

   - **Online Chat**: Use the Apple Support website for live chat options.- download the Apple Support app to access support and schedule repairs.

Frequently Asked Questions

1. **How do I check my MacBook Pro's warranty status?**
   - You can check your warranty status by visiting the Apple Check Coverage page and entering your MacBook's serial number. This will provide you with information about your warranty and eligibility for service.

2. **What should I do if my MacBook won't turn on?**

   o   Try performing a forced restart by holding down the power button for about 10 seconds. If it still won't turn on, connect it to a power source and wait a few minutes before attempting to power it on again. If problems persist, consider contacting Apple Support for further assistance.

3. **How can I improve the battery life of my MacBook Pro?**

   o   To optimize battery life, reduce screen brightness, enable Low Power Mode in the Battery settings, and close unnecessary applications running in the background. Additionally, managing apps that refresh in the background can significantly enhance battery performance.

4. **Can I upgrade the RAM or storage on my MacBook Pro M4?**

   o   The MacBook Pro M4 series features soldered components, meaning RAM cannot be upgraded post-purchase. Storage upgrades are possible through external drives, but internal SSD upgrades are not user-serviceable. Always consider these aspects when configuring your MacBook Pro at the time of purchase.

www.ingramcontent.com/pod-product-compliance
Lightning Source LLC
LaVergne TN
LVHW051716050326
832903LV00032B/4240